The Immodest Hammock

Also by Bill Dodds:
a novel *Twisted Lives*
a collection of poetry *The Almond Tree*

The Immodest Hammock

Bill Dodds

ATQUE

Published by ATQUE

ISBN: 978-0-9559871-2-0

This work is a product of the author's imagination.

Acknowledgements

Thanks to the editors of the following publications in which some of these poems first appeared: *Monkey Kettle and Inclement.*

Contents

I   1

Beware the moss   2

Last letter   3

Fatality   5

Politics   6

Hell   7

Word play   9

Growing   11

The stag   13

Madonna's eyes   14

Two ravens   15

A feminist movement   16

November   17

Crossroads   18

Reformation   19

Orgiva   20

Death   21

She   22

Rebirth   23

Unbounden   24

Tarnished rings   25

The Clapham omnibus   26

Comfort blanket   27

The place   28

The tower   29

An instant   30

Saint Pancras   31

An arrival   32

Being and nothing   33

The old VW camper-van   34

Lunch in Arles   35

Waiting for vegetable stew   36

The immodest hammock   37

II   39

    Plagued by identity   40

    Pretty lady   41

    The collier   42

    Tom Simpson   43

    The charge   45

    Remains   46

    Tea time   47

    Lime Street to Dover Marine via Victoria   48

    The digger   49

    Hope Street Wake   51

    The leavings of Liverpool   53

    The ninety-six   54

    Dissolution   55

    The deal   57

    The business trip   58

    Hard times of old England   59

    Ten   60

    Foreever home   61

    The irregular father   62

    Sunday?   63

    Riddle   64

    Grace   65

    God or nature   66

    Etcetera   67

For the enlightenment of

Robert Fergusson and Adam Smith

I

Beware the moss

Muircheartach! Muircheartach!

'Gaudete,' cried the cross swingeing priest.
'Buaileann mo chroí,' intoned the wandrous bard.

And the sodden moss murmured, 'beware old lords of the Isle.'

Irish paled gallowglass, masters of flesh hacking slaughter,
summoned saffron splashed kerns, breathless,
plashed blackthorn hafted axes and spears,
new laid, hedged against disinterred shot.

A Kingan! A Kingan!

'Feir noch men of weir,' led the bible swigging pastor.
'How lang sall subtill Sathan rage?' rhymed the Christ-cleaved
poet.

And the shaken moss giggled, 'welcome new lords of the Isle.'

Planters spewed powdered lead smoke, strode forward,
knees sank below a bog of fearful once-men,
blood, shite, puke, bone mealed manure,
future nurture for saltired borne crops.

And the crooked moss belched ancient stones from its suppurating
womb.

Last letter

I'm sure you will be happy,
very happy, says he, not
to sound sarcastic, unless
an idealistic type of being,
but when were you ever so?

And I took one road,
and he took another.

Write and tell, how everything
has gone with you and yours,
and tell me deeply how you
feel, I miss your smile, your
bright bored look, one time
inhabitant of these silly walls
of pain, (halls of one's fame).

And I took one road,
and he took another.

Last letter in my pocket,
skim read, unanswered,
far too busy, our ending
unknown, so much time,
to keep in touch, to meet.

And I took one road,
and he took another.

I wanted to write,
can you teach me?
a question of spelling,
letters, words, sentences,
punctuated meanings.

And I took one road,
and he took another.

He published lettered texts,
on a passion we shared,
monasteries of the medieval
mind, words that spoke to me
in the worst of times, thrice.

And I took one road,
and he took another,
and he met death,
an ocean before me.

Fatality

When we first met,
it was a fatal accident,
her eyes danced,
a polka, what a polka,
before she smiled,
a nervous eaten grin,
we met again, again,
but not by any chance,
she knew exactly who I was,
those eyes no longer danced,
they strutted, stared, starred
with unspoken *joie de vivre*,
when we last met,
had been a while,
so much had passed,
so little changed,
she cleaved my skull,
with red ragged love.

Politics

A table set for politics.
besieged by bastards' smiles,
crossed by harlots' hands.

Three children,
eyes wide and open,
glared at those phosphorous flares.

No glasses at the table,
for Lalique to say the grace.
smashed like their skulls.

No wine at the table,
for Lafitte to praise the faith.
spilled like their blood.

Three children,
eyes tight shut,
blind to those hellish-black fires.

Innocents,
betrayed by Pilate's words,
condemned at Jove's command.

Hell

We're all going to hell,
or so a good friend says,
she has it well defined,
and close at hand,
I guess.

But I first saw hell,
ruling in splendour,
an adolescent neck
craned, within a baptistery,
a Florentine mosaic,
to remind the new born,
of self immolation,
if not Godly as scripture,
or deviants from mother's
holier commandments,
yet he seems a friend,
gobbling damned bodies,
legs, like fresh spaghetti,
drooling from his mouth,
and those little devils,
cheeky lads and lasses,
prodding the once joyous,
to bathe in sulphur's pools.

We're all going to hell,
or so a good friend says,
she has it well defined,
and close at hand,
I fear.

And I went to hell once,
not a welcome journey,
not a survival of the soul,
supported by magic charms,
until Thoth weighs the heart,
admits one to the field of reeds,
it was more a trance,
a lack of mindful motion,
black nothingness,
hatred of oneself,
distrust of others,
emotional silence,
a gagged collage,
of all last things,
experienced.

We're all going to hell,
or so a good friend says,
she has it well defined,
and close at hand,
but why?

Word play

We are simple fools,
welded and twisted,
shorn from iron rods.
freedom that is yielded
by the rhythmic hammer,
in the white furnace,
to the beat of a drum.

Promise me this darling,
to sing at my funeral,
a song from your heart,
the lyrics unknowable,
the tune unplayable.

We are a rainbow pattern,
shining in cool water,
drawn from the brook,
ground by the whetstone,
each blade sharpened,
in the swordsmith's hands,
to the strum of a lyre.

Promise me this darling,
to sing at my funeral,
a song from your heart,
the lyrics unknowable,
the tune unplayable.

We are an open secret,
drawn from our sheath,
slaughtering last fears,
harvesting ripe corn,
dripping with blood,
in the warriors hand,
to the shieldwall's chant.

Promise me this darling,
to sing at my funeral,
a song from your heart,
the lyrics unknowable,
the tune unplayable.

We are hidden now,
still tangled together,
stripped of our garnets,
moist with dusk's dew,
nestled like sweethearts,
in the shade of the reed-bed,
to the warbler's song.

Promise me this darling,
to sing at my funeral,
a song from your heart,
the lyrics unknowable,
the tune unplayable.

Growing

As children we played,
our arms outstretched,
finger tips touching,
and then we whirled,
bodies spinning tops,
round and round,
until we fell, dizzy,
laughing and giggling,
lying on the grass,
watching the clouds,
swirling high above,
in the safe blue sky,
ourselves growing.

Thinking ourselves
beyond childhood,
he looks, she looks,
a water mirror
without distortion,
she waves, he waves,
she girlish, he boyish,
arms outstretched,
finger tips touching,
perfume and cologne,
vital adult scents,
our eyes linger,
pale offerings,
dark sacrifice,
yet we still whirl,
minds, not bodies,
with platonic friendship,
with sensual desire,
in a clear night sky.

Demons in the West,
herders of timid souls,
consume our bodies,
swallow our fears,
but puke nothingness,
for the heart's journey
skips past those devils,
now stop thinking and
embrace me.

The stag

Hear the keening women gather,
ears of swaying barleycorn awake
the tears in slumbering cloudy eyes
of gleaners, another summer season,
ewes' milk foams, its grass knotted pots,
in dusks' embers, in the speckled smoke,
night's watchmen, fading before red sun,
the risen flames, from where the river flows,
nearer to the shades of life than lthe deep sleep.

A woman's scream,
on a distant breeze,
born like a May flower,
white apple blossom,
drowned by black rain,
before the bees feed.

Woollen cloaks, plaid hues, stooped shoulders
clasped and pinned by chiselled brooches,
arms heavy with golden twisted bands,
necks bearing beads of jet and amber,
cheeks sad, savaged by raw scratches,
breasts bruised fresh purple, tinged yellow,
auburn hair grisailled with mud and ash,
these three women trail the naked stag,
masked as a silent unmanned scream,
antlers lowered, kneeling before his bier.

An infants new-born cry,
on a distant breeze,
born like a May flower,
white apple blossom,
drowned by black rain,
before the bees feed.

Madonna's eyes

In a crowded, moon lit square,
hot and humid with a stench,
of sanctimonious incense,
a squalid stage erected there,
to host a band of players,
whose hooded acolytes,
sprawl over benches,
and crow from balconies,
the warm up act a monk,
a portly specimen, bald,
a book burner by his hands,
scorched with blackened scars,
he grasps a rosewood crucifix,
held before his tearful eyes,
his blistered mouth snaps open,
Hail Mary seems to be the phrase,
but she no longer sees him,
her poetic joy, her brutal pain,
to find her love is not at home.

Two ravens

Think of myself,
a galleass off Barbary,
oar-less and rudderless,
sails torn by shot,
restless on the tide-less sea.

Think of yourself,
a Spanish Lady
all silver gilt and blue,
eyeless in Sevillian splendour,
deaf to Giralda's peals.

Think of ourselves,
two crucified ravens,
high in the wizard's tower,
waiting for redemption,
to extract the anguished nails.

A feminist movement

Two peacocks
paraded
like queens,
the bikes
whirred fast,
from behind,
forward, past,
racy types,
over King's
queer cobbles,
hair flew,
ribbons of ebony,
golden streamers,
wolf whistled,
twice, a glance
backwards, each
a delight, a lemur's
screech, braked,
smiled, and said,
'Hello.' Twice.

November

All Hallows eve,
All Saints past,
November now,
Book of Hours,
opened, once more
the pruning season,
with sharpened shears,
to lop the branches,
dead wood first,
but then the growth,
cut hard, one two three,
an outward facing bud,
young bleeding sap,
cauterised with tar,
the tree will bear
a sweeter stronger fruit.

Crossroads

On a slight rise with a view of a heavenly spire,
added when fashion dictated in a greyer stone,
across the valley of the Sharn, a clear flowing brook,
an old man picks wild violets, plays she loved me,
minds-eyes the last procession and breathes his youth,
into his smoke scarred lungs and out onto the frost,
rests on his blackthorn stick, cut half a century then,
his lover resting on a cart, shrouded, oxen pulled,
they struggled up that hill, she heavier than a plough,
she remained young, decomposed in a shallow grave,
marked by his memory, alone at the crossroads.

Reformation

In a crumbling, darkling church,
cleansed of reformation white,
drawn to the central triptych,
he contemplates a sunlit hell,
of man's material pleasures,
where monstrous torturers
delight in teasing victims,
whose desire for hedonistic wants
escapes beyond their carnal needs
into an orgy of sadistic splendour.

Love? Compassion? Peace?

A man, a son, deposed,
carried from the cross,
mourned by his friends.

Orgiva

Sun dried, raisins clinging to a Roman vine,
the white drenched houses crushed, span
a shrivelled river, Chico, vapid rocks its water,
heritage preserved, observed, fierce eyes,
ripe skin, Moriscos whose ancestors survived,
remained beyond last resistance to conquistadors,
apostolic monarchs, catholic planters of iron-willed
cathedrals in the shattered soul of Al Andalus.
Olives, almonds, lemons, figs clutter Guadalfeo's plain,
slaves to brusque mountain ranges - Lujar, Alpujarra -
whose snow capped winter peaks store a lifetime,
water funnelled, as almond blossom scents the air,
through ancient channels, down sculptured terraces,
trickles rebirth, whilst generations melt to nothing,
passing beneath a trinity of peaks, towards sunrise,
upwards along a coarse and wondrous path, sunset
within paradise, the liminal walls of the necropolis.

Death

Two legs, displayed apart,
one head thrust between,
drowned in female blood,
self blinded, not shriven,
overseen by his mother,
her wounds borne in sorrows,
before his shrouded corpse.

She

Blind-sighted Homer,
Helen's mystical bard,
bit into a pomegranate,
tasted honey and bile.

Her mortality beckoned him,
her beauty offended him,
she summoned him to speak
to an audience beyond time.

Rebirth

Sad,
stone masked,
she stands alone.

A childish body,
sprawled on shattered sands,
washed by shallow waves.

She gasps,
holds a black eyed marigold,
looks westward.

Reborn,
her ancestral myths,
worship a chastened moon.

Unbounden

Taken at her last sunset,
golden, copper reddened,
mined in Snowdonian hills,
once a fey wedding troth,
became a mourning ring,
which bit too deeply.

At his daughters' insistence,
he tugged and insisted,
dragged past knuckle bone,
left pale banded, impressed hide,
fresh dawns concealed his scar,
and the white hart gasped freedom.

Tarnished rings

Walking together with hesitant steps,
from the half opened supermarket door,
an automatic one, you know that slides,
but pauses in disrespect, contemptuous,
in the humidity of a mid summer's eve,
dusk postponed, and yet the clouds congeal,
and hide the sun, but he glimpses, thrice,
Noah would be proud, which means?
proud of the forming couplet, couple
the young woman's smile, a coy smile,
the man's glance at scuffed loafing shoes,
she black haired, shorts cropped, tanned,
he checks his mobile phone, shows her,
what? but she laughs, touches his arm,
he steps back, waves towards a car,
he steps closer, she steps back a little,
clumsy dancers' steps, her hand offered,
her hand taken, tarnished rings clash,
the watcher closes his eyes, hums a tune,
'We'll gently walk, and sweetly talk,
Till the silent moon shine clearly;
I'll grasp thy waist, and, fondly prest,
Swear how I love thee dearly.' [1]

([1] Quote from Robert Burns: Westlin Winds)

The Clapham omnibus

The person on that Clapham omnibus,
wrapped up warm against tomorrow,
nudged me, 'you know,' she says,
'the Roman arena was hereabouts.'

There the retiarius once chased, hot
for the secutor, across bloody sands,
one first, steps nimble and swift,
the other a stumbling carapace,
perspective shielded by a hoplite's helm,
movement impeded by fine gilded greaves,
engraved with Hermes' magic spells,
sword and shield held forward,wary
of the unpredicted three pronged stabs,
of the shadow swing of lead-weighted net.
but the god of mediocrity laughs,
grinds the soul with sandpaper,
coarsens the ragged edges of joy,
back in the howling arena,
the secutor blinked into the sunlight,
helm removed, her hair cut short.

Comfort blanket

The hidden child
sucks its comfort,
a crazy blanket,
granny's crafted gift,
carried beyond its
adolescent threshold,
a shredded shroud of
skewed words
hidden feelings
misdirected signs,
in consequence,
open doors swing
shut, alone, along
the living corridor,
until tears dissolve
one's final fear.

The place

She suggested the place,
I asked two local girls,
one smiled, one laughed,
as if they knew the score,
an alley near the riverside,
their guttural accents clashed,
I watched them walk away,
skinny jeans, leather boots,
clipped heels against the cobbles,
the costumes of the street,
as if a cold war spy in Paris
I glanced behind, twice,
pushed open the café door,
inside, all stripped pine,
all torn red vinyl seats,
approached the bar,
ordered a café au lait.

The tower

Tongue tied,
fingers twisted,
nudging elbows,
middle aged,
teenage lovers,
on a park bench,
in an industrial town,
gaze through the rain,
at a redeveloped
cast iron tower,
refurbished relic,
of Victorian pride,
waiting for a train,
to take them home.

An instant

A girl, sitting pretty,
across the railway tracks,
in an indefinite cavern,
Baltic blonde?
no darker roots,
nursing a bouquet,
crossed damsel's legs,
pursed powdered mouth,
cool inward eyes,
a train arrives,
blocks the view,
exit stage right.

Saint Pancras

Over in a studied blink,
forty hasty steps beyond
the hollow golden thread,
platform six hundred and sixty-six,
No-where at Saint Pancras,
eleven fifty-five PM,
the demons waltz,
the train don't stop,
the piano player plays,

She's offered up God's acre,
her own green gilded land,
the right to glean the open fields,
secluded pannage for the pigs,
ponds fresh with perch and pike,
a well dug deep into the soul,
nourished by a shining brook.

Platform three,
Some-where in Saint Pancras,
the piano player sings,
she's waiting, restless,
her face explodes,
now joy irradiates,
a half life of eternity,
through a tinted double gaze,
the train does stop.

An arrival

Her head, on his chest, scruffy black hair,
ruck-sac, deserted at his booted feet,
five forty-five pm, about that he thought,
his last half hour, spent, chilled, shuffled,
a double expresso, distended plastic cup,
tossed careless, wandering eyes, shifted
amongst female departures, carrion's eyes.

Her hands pulled at his waist, manicured
nails, polished in the French manner, kissed,
no words, opposites seated at a false café,
aluminium table, toes touched beneath,
his gaze lost now and then, returned to her
bobbed face, she sipped a skinny cappuccino
decorated with a chocolate-powdered heart.

Being and nothing

Across the Pont St Michel,
twin towers of Our Lady,
blessing the couple,
whose shoulders are touching,
to the Départ St Michel,
zinc tables for lovers,
deep in the café,
turned onto each other,
fingertips kissing,
sipping Pernod or Ricard,
washed down with expresso,
the little green fairy,
leads away from the Seine,
along rue St Séverin,
to a grey gothic church,
where they both light a candle,
to the flames of their youth.

That old VW camper-van

Once painted in a gaudy green,
now flayed with rustic patina,
not a welcome state of corrosion,
salvaged at its irregular borders,
where verdigris rivets scattered,
immodest in its display of decay,
copper, bronze, iron, and lead,
oxidised by climatic changes,
its unpolished bonnet scarred
by rivulets of dry acerbic sweat,
streaks of raw umber, burnt sienna,
smear windows that gape to expose,
anonymous residues of future lives.

Lunch in Arles

A pavement brasserie,
next to a santon seller,
opposite the arena,
tables and chairs,
spill onto the street,
salade Niçoise for her,
salade rustique for him,
a tourist's pichet for both,
rosé for her, red for him,
his teeth strip a black olive,
she shares a fresh anchovy,
cream plates on checked cloth,
mopped clean with stale bread,
she in cut down jeans and smock,
he in sandals, shorts and tee,
she first, lithe legs stretched,
he watches, watches, follows,
up to a ferocious blue sky,
perched on worn stone steps,
two wriggling bums,
two twisting necks,
two grasping hands,
one luxurious kiss.

Waiting for vegetable stew

Cross-legged, sat in gravel grey dust,
skirt Provençal, a cheap and gaudy weave,
broad swirling stripes, madder red, saffron yellow,
its hem pulled down below her knees, so girl-like,
head stooped, chin tucked in, but only a little,
gaze resting on a broken paper backed romance,
tongue licked lips, miming unleavened words,
steps from sneakier clad feet across the square,
she squints beyond the plane tree umbrella,
its shadow draws the naked outline of her breasts,
bold beneath a lace trimmed cotton camisole,
book dropped, arms stretched, he pulls her to her feet.

The immodest hammock

A hammock strung between two poplar trees,
looking past their boughs to Mont Ventoux,
whose whitened whale bone summit blinding harsh
against the vision of the waves she formed,
by her hesitant strokes, by her splashing feet,
breaking the water, mazed with early evening sun.

A stone cracked bread oven, fired with rosemary twigs,
hollowed peppers smouldering on the griddle pan,
courgettes, prepared, chopped and oiled,
speckled with salt and crushed black pepper,
scarlet tomatoes sliced and strewn with basil leaves,
two cracked glass tumblers, filled with Côte du Luberon.

She pushes upwards, hands splayed pool-side,
a false start, falling backwards, the surface cracks,
her shoulders rock, laughing, she tries again,
rises from her ocean, clambers on all fours,
her shortish hair slicked back, wet down her neck,
a modest stripy towel wrapped round her waist.

His eyes have opened, fingers rough his hair,
he glances to the barbecue, she smiles as
water drips to mark her progress up the steps,
a lilac bush, she sniffs its scent, smiles at its bees,
his eyes have closed again, she's opened hers,
she sings, the hammock sways from side by side.

II

Plagued by identity

The vestry door half open,
a tallow candle burns,
a thumb's length from its root,
the parish clerk sits at his desk,
recording burials, not births,
etching a pool of blackness,
in formulaic schoolboy Latin,
unlearned man, he mimics
the priest's deft strokes,
spreads sand to blot the page,
closes the book and sighs,
steps out of the church porch,
watches the plague diggers
swiftly spread quick lime.

The microfilm reader purrs,
each page a murky photocopy,
silver grained secretary script
gives way to slovenly scrawl,
the man magnifies the text,
leans forward and peers,
his eyes screwed, tired
of listless, blank words,
linked by a common name,
a surfeit of romantic poetry
recreates imagined lives,
but nowhere does it talk,
of his life, of his loves,
only of his burial in 1666.

Pretty lady

A photograph,
of Ilford colours,
faded into grey,
her silvered hair,
long down her back
brushed as a youth
a démoiselle,
so still in that
calm open coffin,
set against the wall,
for a trembling,
little errand boy,
to glimpse on tiptoes
his first contented
corpse.

In a mission church
memorial Sunday,
he visited the spoil,
covering her grave,
in the subsidence
of a colliery's
bone-yard.

The collier

Blue black scarred lads,
early schooled to coal's blasted underworld,
blind, obedient follow the seaward seam.

New terraces, brick built,
welcome family men, still country aired
graze pigs, goats, hens on village green.

Half a man's height,
Harvey stands, roof of sodden stone,
lime hard water slakes its thirsty, naked men.

Eight hundred feet
full bitter floods, no pumps restrain the tide,
three years closed, men flee south or take the dole.

Water dammed, defeated,
more hours, less pay, deeper shafts to narrower seams,
No Gala, Nineteen Twenty Six, lock out, strike, depression.

Bright young things dance,
war's rhythm inspires a few to Spain, the rest to Hitler's war,
old colliers remain, joined by young lads, all marrows now.

Retired unstooped to council house,
he walks the mile, drags on a fag, sups a slow pint, bides his time,
Great North Road unites: children visit, golden wedding, death.

Head stones bowed
eastward facing, across the grassed spoiled land,
cracked by sixty years of greed, not nature, not God's design.

Tom Simpson

The tree lined climb begins,
twisting beyond Bedoin,
upwards to Mont Ventoux,
a car tinted and air conditioned.

How did he die?
booze and pills,
but even so,
this gentle, shaded climb,
hors catégorie?

Our picnic, insects dance
on pâté and brie,
sweating muscles,
cycling eyes intent
on road's imagined yellow,
in their dreams of Tom, of glory.

We pack, and pass them,
pull them higher,
the landscape flayed of trees ,
a white obscenity
of broken rocks,
viscious mirrors of the sun,
regard the black rider,
Tom's granite heir.

Husband and father,
he fell, regained his seat,
blind sight betrayed him,
three kilometres left,
a bed of fractured stones,
oxygen is scarce,
scarcer in Tom's lungs.

That night he rests,
compartment number three,
the morgue, Saint Marthe Hôpital,
le Tour rolls on, fourteenth stage,
a British victory,
the peloton mourns,
Tom honours them,
his hymn, their will to win.

Yellow, green, polka dot,
speed, testosterone, doped blood.

The charge

Packed behind the imaginary milk filled syringe,
rainbows of jerseys, testosterone ridden men,
muscled, tanned black, dirty black with wind,
sun and air, empty starless stares, enlivened
by the passage of a cruising senorita, busking
for café society, arses needled, pin cushioned
to inject speed, to dominate the mind, to crank
the highest gear, upwards to a mountain finish,
where oxygen is scarce, tablets concealed, ever
ready for the last domestic charge to sixtieth place.

Opposite a different pack, a line of girls and boys,
waving, strung out across the blistered tarmac road,
placards daubed in protest, homage to their friend,
murdered by police, yesterday, at night, in the dark,
stabbed, their rage, their innocence, their class,
angry flashes of steel mirrored their radical hatred
that afternoon, flames reaped corn fed fields,
rats danced, but no pied piper, the peloton fled,
race abandoned, charged still, contracts fulfilled,
in hotel bars, they heard the students scream.

Remains

The football passed from
left foot to right foot, trapped
a smile, not knowing sadness,
a grandson and a granddad,
whose parchment skin,
hollow cheeks,
narrowed waist,
a palimpsest,
a doom.

Neat and tidy front room,
a widowed sister sobs,
a grandson hides behind the sofa,
later explores the house and finds,
white Russian sabre,
million rouble promise,
masonic apron, blue and white,
illuminated retirement scroll,
granted two short years ago.

Tea time

Head strong long brewed leaf tea,
dished in crazy willow pattern.

Tough muscled oxtail soup,
laced with ladled Cyprus sherry.

Plate plied with shin of Irish beef,
mellowed in a marble safe,
twice daubed, slow brazing,
potatoes fed by meagre gravy,
chains of shredded cabbage,
gems of pickled onions,
Lea and Perrins sauce.

So, on another wintry day,
honeycomb of dreamy tripe,
pools filled with sweeter milk,
circled by dunes of buttery mash.

Burnt umber skinned rice pudding,
clotted cream beneath the crust,
dollops of tarter apple stew,
tempered with Demerara sugar.

Head strong long brewed leaf tea,
dished in crazy willow pattern.

Lime Street to Dover Marine via Victoria

A splash of dawn yellow through dirty glass,
crowded out, off the Lime Street train,
He pushed through mourning commuters,
striving to shave ten minutes,
from a tepid, workday feast,
fated for the City, shops, cafés.

Bulked double by cavernous rucksack,
packed by mother, socks paired, ironed pants,
an extra fiver stuffed in sweating hand,
embarrassed by an Imperial Leather kiss,
dad's hands behind his back,
he coughed, twice.

'Fuckin students, work for a living,'
whined one Kentish man,
whose elbow struck my face,
a momentary redness of shock,
an unwelcome shiver of recession,
an incentive to compete.

Ticket shown, old fashioned compartment,
dust stuffed seat, stiff sliding door, heat,
departed, the boat train to Dover Marine,
slow past blue-rinse get on your bike graffiti,
his torn overcoat a crumpled pillow,
his head against the shuddering window.

He read *'Le Tartuffe.'*

The digger

Mackets Lane, Hillfoot, Ford Road, Ward Blenks,
smelled the rancid crispy, inhaled ammonia,
crossed Mersey's bridge, by West Bank industry,
on his bike, a day's sunshine in a rainy summer.

A tanned overseer, beneath the castle rock,
explained the task, introduced his underseer,
bell tight-bottomed flares, string-dyed tee,
handed out the trowels, placed him a metre square.

A ruddy earth, sand soft soil exposed
beneath the turf stripped ancient plough soil,
he scraped the surface, metronome strokes, a hand's
width broad, revealed white clay debris of a drag.

First trophy, in a sixteenth century layer, bagged,
packed lunch, golden wonder crisps, tap water,
eaten in ship lapped, tiled barn, with other volunteers,
paid a labourer's daily rate by Manpower's Services.

The underseer smiled, and offered him a smoke,
shake of his head, a grimaced leer, she smiled again,
sucked him to her: sweat stained shirt, slight breasts,
dark eyes, close enough to see a chipped front tooth.

Sun stinging his neck, undressed that metre square,
my lozenge trowel churned out a green glazed lip,
she sat, cross-legged with him, held hands to guide
the way, a few millimetres revealed, he smelt her scent.

Next day it rained, the first Crossville bus had failed
to come, the next, standing only until West Bank,
then the remnant of a seat, next to an engrossed man,
who sniffled through a Yate's wine-lodged purple nose.

The overseer lectured in the barn of unrealised dreams,
crop marked wartime photos from the air, his evidence,
no documents, no artefacts, but they will be revealed.
'Keeps him off the dole,' he thought. 'Buys my next pint.'

He had sat behind her on our straw baled benches,
envied the shadow of a strap beneath her linen smock,
and conscious of an adolescent gaze, she swayed her head,
played with her walnut hair, gave him a half tuned smile.

Back in the trench, her scent again, soft palm on shoulder,
breath on neck's standing hairs, behind him, he stood, turned,
she squatted, outlined a dark crescent, with a slender finger,
'A post hole,' she said. 'I'll trowel now, watch me.'

Hope Street Wake

The stakes are high,
father and son,
they hope, await
the call, hushed voices
mean malignant.

Nurses preach,
a perfect scar,
the best I've seen,
rays burnish hope
of remission.

The consultant,
offers her warm coat,
leads to the door,
with wintry smile
displays no hope.

Sandstone, concrete,
cathedrals watch,
in Hope Street's wake,
dead cities, where
her forebears wait.

Her brother flies,
five thousand miles,
eternity in mind,
moist eyes betray
the next reunion.

Her breath is weak,
her hunger fled,
all hope deceased,
the broken voice,
death in her sleep.

Is she still here?
he kneels beside,
sweet Irish brogue,
Hurley shoulders,
heavy with tears.

Intercessions,
God, Holy Saints,
behind her now,
a priest prays,
mumbles requiat.

Nan blind, rages,
milk soured by loss,
survived them all,
damns doctors,
once more, too late.

Father tallies
morphine fed pills,
all untouched,
belie her pain,
his consolation.

Son wanders
through that maze,
of dead bureaucracy,
his sorrow mislaid,
beyond the open grave.

Too wise to mourn,
his grief postponed
for twenty years,
mad, foolish now,
what hewed his tears?

The leavings of Liverpool

Remembered seasons, tramping urban fields,
grey pebble-dashed , semi detached suburban clerks,
flaking sandstone villas, bed-sits for inner city poor,
sat on garden walls, watched the old couple, kissed a girl.

Shuffled through turnstiles, crushed kopites,
ludi ludorum, sive panis et circenses,
those European nights, whose floodlit stars
sheltered Liver reds from rock hard desperation.

On buses home, the illusion died, children conceived,
surrounded by ill-famed towers, busted heirs of rational plans,
high in that blackened red sky, litter strewn, condompathways,
as drug sodden as were vintage dockland drinking dens.

The bird watched sons beg for work on ship-less, wharves,
luckier sons had spurned the Mersey, found factory jobs in Speke,
eight hour shifts, paid overtime, Costa Blanca holidays,
mortgages, neat pruned lawns and modish anaglypta walls.

Eleven-plus children aspired to red brick first degrees,
remembered jobless summers, factory gate refusals,
saw parents work short time, school friends down the social,
dentists, teachers, lawyers relived the leavings of Liverpool.

The ninety-six

Red ribboned mummers chanted,
herded like condemned beasts,
by black liveried babewyns,
marshalled by misrule,
with smeared copper hats,
and plague doctors' beaks,
and savage wood shafts,
shunted through death's tunnel,
into the light, on Lepping Lane,
penned by strained steel wire,
painted in owlish club colours,
concentrated, pressed, pinned
against that savage safety-fence,
denied sanctuary to the east,
by fate-guarded, locked gates,
limbs paralysed, eyes sightless,
lungs failed, the ninety-six died.

Dissolution

Today the carer nodded,
unlocked her door,
assured them of integrity,
regretted disinfectant
wished them well, no rush.

Five years past she,
read the Mirror,
watched Corrie on TV,
two black plastic bags,
folded, laid on the one
stripped naked bed.

Four years gone-by,
sherecognised the kids,
smiled and joked,
old worn clothes
in the wardrobe,
wasted keep-sakes
in the chest of draws.

Three years now, she
asked when will he
be home for tea, for tea,
an inlaid box,
a wedding ring,
a press report
of his demise.

Two years, she
she called his name,
wanted him to take her
to the Grafton Rooms,
suit-cased photos
of the mourned,
husband, mother.

Last visit, she
kissed her mum's
chapped lips, held
her claw-like hand,
'When's the next tram
home, to Picton Clock?
Where am I? Who am I?'

The deal

Heads of agreement, not agreed,
but time is of the essence,
to hand over, to deliver,
people, assets, buildings,
essential skills, a trade
sale of public service futures,
improvements at no cost.

Root out the drones,
keep only busy bees,
who'll do two jobs for one,
how else will public profits flow,
to pay for cars, sharp managers,
for bonus pool and dividends,
doe eyed hyena of private equity.

Who says it's borrowed money?
I have it here, the balance sheet,
freshly laundered linen, plush carpets,
look share capital fully paid, no doubts,
vintage wine, black buttered skate, sorbet,
forget due diligence, no need, good chaps,
pass the port, light my cigar, do the deal.

The business trip

Early start, sat neat, suited, booted, glanced
through smeared front window, stomach
churned rhubarb yoghurt, free of fats, natural,
car engine, sporty, soft top, sighed, orange,
personal number, plate smile, ace, king, queen,
jack unzipped, leave the coffee - half emptied,
on board sat. nav. chatters, interrupts, small talk,
business conversation, bawdy gossip, is she really,
of course he is, turgid repetition of who they'd
meet, snippets of names – spouse, children, age –
short in memory, as if they know, like them even,
not late, despite the sat. nav's detour to avoid,
each presented, a unique selling point of view,
appetising price, florid achievements, intoned sermons
in a torpid smoke filled room, this was long ago,
on a hot day, in a hot town, nowhere in particular,
decision over, reinforced with owlish shrieks, over
Abigail's buffet lunch, always used for special days,
value for money, cheapest eh, Ayckbourn chatter,
fast journey home, one stop somewhere, coffee.

Hard times of old England

They laughed at the old drunken jokes,
told against their middle class selves,
for some a lifetime's venal office work,
for others borrowed from a royal bank,
trapped, a lifestyle choice, uncomfortable?
semi detached marriage vows, work widow,
botox widower, kids grown up, grandchildren?
welcomed for a holiday by the wine dark sea,
they remembered their sixties, golden years?
sit ins at the LSE, Garden House riots, traitor,
Dylan's changing times, Joni's Chelsea mornings,
an afternoon fucking, slender bodies then, firm,
now paunched and pinched, his dreary countdown
to retirement, a flattering leaving speech, applause,
flowers for her undoubted loyalty, a cheesy kiss,
her sickening realisation that he's home for good,
thank God for golf, rotary, and the masonic hall.

Ten

Smelt the sweetness, saw his breathless
stare, stepped back, ignored an offered hand
his shrunken face, worn too long, old razor,
nicked chin, flask poured coffee gripped,
official coffee vile, six months ago he said,
preferred his finely ground, a domestic brew,
stumbled over excised words, claimed elbow,
walked to the car, his old bag, clutched,
boxed black case of a scuffed friendship,
silent drive, open back door, counted to ten,
neat bottles, empty on the kitchen floor.

Forever home

He works from home,
spare bedroom office,
space for desk, a base
PC, six tabs opened,
none work related,
he emailed her,
'Jesus! there's
a recession,
you know that.'

Scatter cushions,
double income
no kids and young,
forever young,
before the clock,
tic toc, tic toc,
crocodile rocks
Peter and Wendy,
mortgage rates at
two percent, and banks
bought clothes and cars,
when life was free and
work a place to breath,
home an Indian, a
transient rented flat.

She messaged him
the latest news,
last status update
the battery failed,
'the van is here
time now to leave
the forever home,
I'll text you later,
shit no credit left.'

The irregular father

Not an odd day,
here and there
a flexi day? no,
not annual leave,
used up to avoid
hidden robbery,
an end of year cull.

Not a few days
paternity leave,
whilst mother
suckles new
borne babe,
he undertakes his
household chores.

Now every day,
the walk,
four times,
ten minutes,
down the hill,
hand held, hopping,
puddle splashing.

The school gate,
the guarded wait,
the feminine crowds,
huddled powdered faces,
suspicious inward looks,
who dares to catch the eye
that irregular father?

Sunday?

Urban four-by-fours, gathered early doors,
forty shilling freeholders, all come to vote
for specials, top ten wines, three a tenner,
save one hundred pounds each calendar year,
a camp young man, with glad elder mentor,
wrapped arms with civil ringed delight,
a boozed stomach, veined nose, of a certain age,
a wife, with neat French nails and studded jeans,
a toddler pulled mother, her milk stained blouse,
a sign for a newly borne, a cradle capped darling.

All present, cards at the tills, trolley laden,
want cash, desire honeyed financial products,
neat insurance cover, sour tasting car loans,
machine gunned, bleeped, attuned to swipe
of plastic magnetic stripe, white needles,
violent light devoid of sympathetic spectrum,
at rainbow's end the febrile scribbler sips
on a tepid latte con lecche, and munches
on a croissant, an almond one, what else?

Riddle

Entranced, tweeting on the mobile,
Apologia pro vita sua on the desk,
blonde streaked student, brows plucked,
ears plugged, IPOD whitened teeth,
nails, purple puce, tapping notebook keys,
unstifled yawn, eyes wander to a nicer arse,
round and round the reading room,
where Wittgenstein, once thought?
English now, accented lingua franca,
he hears *Ich heise* or *Ich liebe*, he's unsure,
he doesn't hear the name or the reply,
he waits without grace or patience,
for his withdrawal from the stacks.

Grace

Yesterday's arrival,
a brown envelope,
a nervous eye,
Ulster post marked,
an unwelcome message,
death or illness?
a hasty scribble,
thin red handed,
my address in ink,
neater, cursive inside,
presbyter black,
recognisable scripture,
through decades of
Christ's greetings,
good news for the elect
of unmet children,
ancestral names,
who criss-crossed
the narrow Irish Sea,
avoiding earthly purgatory,
Calvin's predestined few,
free to contemplate philosophy,
to search for the flirtatious lights
beyond the dancing shadows.

God or nature

Changed the flowers on dad's grave,
turned the hyacinth bulbs to the wall,
threw dry remnants in the council bin,
green lidded for recycling organic stuff,
brushed grass mowing from the stone,
potted the yellow and white daffs, fresh
cut from his back garden, short stemmed,
stunted bulbs from last year's planting,
mum's remembered on the marble too,
buried her elsewhere, two hundred miles
north west, black granite, gold lettered rock,
space unfulfilled for dad's eternal rest.

He contemplates, Calpino's ecumenical cross,
his beliefs, float in an ocean, not a sea of faith,
a friend said once, no broad church could hold her,
added alas? Or was that his imagining? Jung had it
right, wholly reasonable logic can leave mighty
chasms in modern souls, replaced by Marxism,
human rights, or green thoughts, mostly gift
wrapped in self-centred, material nothingness,
God or nature his euphemistic self defence,
before he died, dad had tasted the bread and wine,
refused since mum's canker ridded God from mind.
'I feel like a proper Christian again,' he said.

Etcetera

Look for the evidence,
seek and you will find,
truth is made or broken,
prey for the cleverest mind.

www.ingramcontent.com/pod-product-compliance
Lightning Source LLC
LaVergne TN
LVHW021135080426
835509LV00010B/1359

* 9 7 8 0 9 5 5 9 8 7 1 2 0 *